How To Start Your Own Cosmetic Line

The Brutally Honest Truth From

A Cosmetic Chemist

By

Ginger King

TABLE OF CONTENTS

INTRODUCTION

Billions of dollars flood the cosmetics industry each year. Creams, lotions, lipsticks and mascaras come in an endless varieties to meet the desires and needs of every type of consumer. What satisfies the consumer searching for organic or natural products may not satisfy one looking for scientifically-driven and cutting-edge ingredients. If you enjoy cosmetics, and have an entrepreneurial spirit, ingenuity, style and business savvy, in this book you will learn how to start your own skin/hair line from home to scale up, how to create your makeup line and much more.

Why am I writing this e-book? Because everyone has a dream, a dream of making people looking and feeling better, a dream of self-accomplishment, and a dream of making a name for yourself. If you fit in these categories, welcome. If you want to learn how to create your own cosmetic line for the sheer pleasure of making money, you may be on the wrong boat. Every business takes sweat equity to make it work. If you do not love the beauty business, your business will not sustain. So for starters, you must have a passion for beauty before you read on.

What qualifies me to write such an e-book? I have been in the beauty business for over 20 years. My experience includes cosmetic formulation, packaging, product development, manufacturing, raw material sales, retail sales, blogging and e-commerce with startups and fortune-500's cosmetic companies. I have embraced the 360's of beauty and love to share with like- minded people. I receive inquiries almost daily on how to start a beauty business. Most of the people want to do it to solve their own problems. Mind you that your problem may not be other's problems. Most of the people also get scared when they hear my brutally honest opinion on how much it will cost them to pursue their dreams.

If you are still with me at this point, congratulations, let's get started!

HOW TO START A SKIN/HAIR LINE FROM HOME?

A homemade cosmetics line can be the perfect way to turn a hobby into a full- or part-time income stream. Whether you choose to focus on hair, skin care or makeup, you'll need to begin by identifying your target market, and their specific cosmetic needs. The beauty care industry is trend driven. Stay well-informed about popular ingredients and products to attract customers through extensive reading and research. Focus on unique properties of your cosmetics to sell them to customers.

So how do you go about having your very own cosmetic business? Follow these steps:

- **Apply for a Federal Tax Identification number for your business**. You need to get all the legal requirements out of the way. Sites like www.legalzoom.com is a good starter to get your company incorporated.

- **Choose a name for your cosmetic line.** Make sure you do a trademark search to ensure the name is not taken. I have seen too many companies changing names after their launch simply because they did not do their homework. Some of you want to be in beauty to have a name for yourself. Perhaps you are a celebrity make-up artist or hair stylist, your name has some recognition to it. However, it is usually not advisable to name a company after a person's name for longevity sake. What if something happened to you down the road, who will take over

6

the business and still run your brand identity? When you want to sell the company for any reason, the new investors may not want to take YOUR name. So think thoroughly about this. Another caveat is if you sell your company to others, you cannot use your own name for another cosmetic line. So think twice!

- **Decide on a business entity for your company**. Generally speaking it can be advantageous to establish your cosmetic company as a limited liability corporation, or as a partnership. Visit the Business Structure page on the U.S. Small Business Administration website to learn about different business entities and their tax implications. Consult with an attorney for advice about business entities and for assistance filing paperwork to establish your business structure.

- **Order equipment and tools to make your cosmetics**. The basic equipment you need includes pots, measuring utensils, heat-safe bowls and spoons, glass or metal beakers and a precision kitchen scale. Store your cosmetic equipment in a separate cabinet from your kitchen equipment.

- **Shop for ingredients for your cosmetics**. Purchase ingredients you can find regularly at an affordable price. You can find many natural oils and herbal ingredients through wholesale cosmetic suppliers, and even on local supermarket shelves. Buy a mini-fridge to store perishable ingredients, such as plant-based oils, separate from your food supply.

- **Write formulas for your cosmetic products**. Make sure you have exact measurement on what you use. Not a pinch of this and a pinch of that type of formulation as your formulas MUST be able to REPRODUCE for quality reasons. Additionally how you process the formula, the temperature and the mixing speed are also important. Detail everything for your formula including where you get your raw materials as Company A's honey may react differently than Company B's honey.

- **Order packaging**. You will need jars, bottles and tubes or your products. Make test batches using your formulas. Give test products to friends and ask them for feedback on the feel and quality of the product. You can get generic packaging from packaging clearance houses such as www.sks.bottle.com

- **Use feedback to fine tune your formulas.** After your creation, you want to sample a few of the "TARGET" market, not everyone you contact with. For example, if the product is intended for use for dry skin type, do not give to your acne-prone teenagers to try. It may seem common sense but a lot of people simply pass on to friends and families who have a face without taking consideration of who the product is for. Always have your target market in mind. If you are developing hair care, make sure you give products to the right demographic to test. If needed, you can even use a mannequin head to play pretty much like how a cosmetologist will when they practicing their crafts.

- **Design labels for your product line and have they printed**. Information that should appear on your product labels includes the net weight, volume and list of ingredients. Refer to the Cosmetic Label Guide on the U.S. Food and Drug Administration website to ensure that your product labels include the appropriate information.

- **Purchase general and products insurance to protect your business from liability or loss.** Compare quotes from several insurance agents to get the best rates for insurance. Refer to the Permit Me tool on the U.S. Small Business Administration website to find authorities that govern businesses in your jurisdiction. Contact your local zoning authority to ensure you can run a small manufacturing operation in your home. Arrange your home manufacturing space and have it inspected if your local regulations require it, before you launch your product line.

- **Create a website for your cosmetic line**. Include original content about your philosophy of beauty care. Set retail and wholesale prices for your products. Include detailed information about your ordering process. Add shopping cart functionality and shipping rate information to your website if you plan to sell directly to retail buyers online. Invite wholesale buyers to contact you for price quotes.

- **Rent a table at a local farmers' market or conventions** .Introduce your product line to shoppers in your community. Invite shoppers to sample your products. Have a supply of sample-sized products to distribute to shoppers. Contact editors at local newspapers about your product and ask them to write a feature article about your business. Visit area boutiques and talk to owners about carrying your product lines in their stores.

All of the above you are doing is simply to "test the market" to see how your creation fare in the public eyes. When you have overwhelmed response and absolutely need to scale up; i.e. find a contract manufacturer to help you with mass quantities (such as minimum order of 5000 pieces), this is when you really need an industry consultant to guide you through the jungles. Your formulas may also be subjected to further refinement and the proper stability, micro, packaging testing as well as repeated insult patch test (RIPT).

HOW TO START A MAKE-UP LINE?

I separated the cosmetic business into skin/hair vs make-up line as they are different animals. Granted there are skin care products that have some color properties and vice versa, the makeup line is a general descriptor of anything that involves highly pigmented materials. It is way easier to create home-made skin, hair or personal products but not color cosmetics. The reason is color cosmetic usually involves many pigments which requires special roller mills and some requires specific pressing machines for eyeshadows and such. Color cosmetics also tend to be very messy and can take up more time to clean than to actually make it. So, if you are still in desire to have your makeup line, here are some tips:

- **Look for wholesalers**. Check online sources to determine where you can obtain makeup wholesale. Several wholesalers have makeup products with no label and will be the basics for your line. This is the easiest way to do.

- **Figure out which type of makeup you want to use in your line**. Some will begin with a few products and then branch off from there. You must have a unique difference that will draw people to your product line.

- **Create formulas with a factory or a consultants**. Try to come up with something unique in the world of makeup to give you an edge in this competitive market. You must be prepared to have 5000 piece minimum for production.

Bottom-line: This is not where you want to DIY especially when there are regulations on what colorants can be used and what colorants can't for safety reasons. Moreover, when it comes to make-up, you must create multiple shades to satisfy the market.

On Develop Your Makeup Brand:

- Come up with a name for the makeup line that is attractive and will make those who buy makeup not only think about your line, but remember it as well. If you are attached to any celebrities, it's an added bonus. It can help but it is not a guarantee to success.

- Create eye catching artwork and designs for the labels and other marketing campaigns.

- Be sure to trademark creative artwork, logos and slogans that are used for your products to prevent theft of intellectual property.

- Promote the brand through marketing efforts. It is a good idea to announce the brand before it actually reaches the market. This is called "pre-sell", which you can determine the demand of your products and have a better idea on how much products you should order from the contract manufacturers or wholesalers.

Do Marketing Survey on Clients Most Likely to Use Your Products.

- Perform a marketing survey of your potential customers.

- Offer incentives, such as a free trial offer of the makeup, to those who are most likely to purchase.

- Understand how to advertise to the target market once this is established and do not just concentrate your efforts off line.

Learn How to Sell Makeup.

- Approach department stores with the makeup line in an effort to get them to carry your line. There should be something different about the makeup you are offering that makes it stand out among others. Those who market to department stores usually have a larger company with attractive packaging and a high mark-up.

- Consider a multi-level marketing plan in an effort to distribute the makeup to clients. This is an ideal way to get started if there is not a lot of money in the business or a solid reputation. Home parties and internet sales can help a makeup line begin to grow.

- Approach those who use makeup in their own business. This can range from makeup artists in studios as well as in beauty shops. When just beginning with a line, it is easier to get established by allowing a beauty salon use your products.

- Establish a fee percentage for the makeup line. Those who use the line in their own business, such as a salon, should have to pay for the products at a discount. This not only helps you sell the line, but also promotes your brand.

- Continue to look for clients for your makeup line. Do not sign an exclusive contract for the brand unless you plan to sell the entire line. The more people who use the makeup line, the more recognizable the brand will become to others.

While it is harder to create a makeup line, the selling of make-up is actually more fun as people like to experiment with new products. Unlike skin care, people do not have as much brand loyalty to color cosmetics as long as it looks good and it has "long wear" quality. For this reason, 8 out of the 10 new cosmetic business tend to be in makeup!

Other tips to consider:

- Search Thomasnet.com or Cosmeticindex.com to find private label manufacturers to supply cosmetics. The websites list the names of hundreds of cosmetics suppliers, and give short overviews of the services they offer.

- Call the companies that provide the products you need. Private label cosmetic suppliers will have stock recipes for products, and may provide a consultant to help you produce custom product formulations.

- Contact a graphic designer to create a logo. Confirm artwork requirements with your cosmetics suppliers.

- Meet with a lawyer and start the process to trademark your business name and logo. With so many products on the market, having a trademark will give your cosmetics line a distinct identity.

- Order your cosmetics. Private label companies have minimum quantity or minimum dollar requirements for your opening order.

- Set up a mini-boutique in an existing store or beauty salon, or rent a kiosk at a mall to sell your cosmetics. Alternately, contact cosmetics buyers at stores you want to carry your cosmetics line. Offer to deliver products for them to sample to entice them to place an order.

HOW TO START A NATURAL & ORGANIC LINE?

About 80% of the clients come to me always start with this sentence: I want to create a chemical-free, natural and organic line. Sure, it sounds GREAT but there are many issues!

First of all, there is no definition of natural or organic by FDA. There are many marketing companies tried to certify ingredients to be natural. Even with certification, they still allow up to 5% synthetic materials. So, the definition of natural products is depending on what association you want to follow? Eco-cert? Cosmos? NPA? USDA Organic?

Secondly, as a cosmetic chemist, I get very ticked off when people say I want chemical-free. Everything is a chemical. As long as you can draw the chemical structure, it is a chemical. Water is H2O. Water is a chemical. What you are really asking is "SAFE" materials. Is it SAFE.

Third of all, natural does not equate safe. I had a client insisting of using certain essential oil as it is natural and supposed to be so good for the skin. When she received the material, she applied on the face and got a big rash. Isn't poison ivy natural?

Fourthly, are you really in for the better of consumers or blindly following the FREE-OF trend? These days, the FREE-OF claims are so prevalent partly because retailers also think that's what consumers want. As long as you slap on a Gluten-Free, Sulfate-Free type of label, it will sell. The joke is if you are going to find salt in the sugar, of course it's salt-free!

Among all the Free-Of claims, the only one I buy into is Paraben-Free. It's not necessary because parabens are bad or it will be banned already. It's because there are studies shown parabens do cause skin irritation. In fact, in Japan, people use methyl-paraben as a marker to test skin sensitivity for "stinging". For that reason, I am in with the crowd.

Recently there are bans on the microbeads (Polyethylene) commonly used in facial or body scrubs. It is not necessary because it's not a good material, but it's not biodegradable for the ecosystem. So for that reason, it is now banned from using it. However for our skin, it does no harm but to help mechanically exfoliate the dead skin layers away.

I encourage marketers when you are making "Free-Of" claims, make sensible ones. Free-of claims do not make your brand more natural. Natural products do not mean better and safer even though there is the trend going for it. The proper way we should ask is it SAFE? I much prefer to follow the EWG (Environmental Working Group) on the chemical classification than blindly formulating products just using natural extracts. So, are you still interested in natural and organic products with potential irritants or safe and non-toxic products?

If you are still interested in Natural & Organic products due to market pressure, here are few tips:

- **Start with an above average budget for development.** Due to the documentation required and specific suppliers you have to use and allocation of storage areas for natural products, be prepared to pay for two times more of the typical cost of goods. You are not adding extra value to the product to consumers but adding costs to yourself for the paper work required.

- **Use fragranced water instead of fragrance.** Fragrance is the number cause of allergy due to the complexity of materials used to create such compound. There are products like fragrance water, which is a blend of fragrant botanicals preserved in glycerin. Your ingredient listing will show up as a bunch of botanical extracts instead of calling it a FRAGRANCE and marketing-wise, it is Fragrance-Free.

- **Avoid of PEG containing products.** PEG stands for Polyethylene Glycol. It can be irritating to the skin. Many of the so-called natural products still contain this material as an emulsifier to help stabilize the cream. There are ways to get around such as choosing eco-certified emulsifier system.

- **Acceptance of natural characteristics.** Natural products are not quality controlled. The quality depends on the weather, the harvest season and a whole other hosts of factors. You cannot expect batch to batch consistency. Natural products also are not as silky and elegant as they cannot contain silicone- the mother horse of all things beautiful. Sure there are substitutes but no substitute can be as close to silicone itself. Having said this, do not kill yourself over when your product does not have the luxurious feel of a silicone containing product. You can be 80% there but an apple pear is never an apple.

WHAT ARE THE STARTUP COSTS?

Starting your own skincare line from home can be profitable, but how quickly profitable is where it gets sticky. If you are a small shop starting out, it is unlikely that you are going to get your products into major retail stores or even midsized local stores. Your best bet is to begin online where you can build some sales data which you can then take to your local markets to convince them to carry your product. If you take the online route, your key start-up costs will be in three primary areas including product development, marketing, and business expenses.

Of course, these costs can vary widely depending on the formulations you are making but here is a minimum general ballpark for what you can expect.

Product development costs

When people think of starting their own cosmetic line, the product development costs are what they generally think about. Basically, these costs include anything related to creating your product such as raw material costs, packaging, and labeling. It also includes the cost of production activities such as mixing the materials together and filling them into the packaging. Cosmetic formulations can run anywhere from $0.10 per pound to $3 per pound but on average you can guess products will cost about $1 per pound. Packaging & labeling will cost another $1 per unit. Add in production and filling costs and your average per bottle cost will be about $2 – $3 per unit.

But you can't just make a few bottles at a time as you'll have to buy minimum quantities of the raw materials and bottles. To get the costs to $2 – $3 per unit you are going to have to make a minimum of 1000 — 5000 units. If you make less your costs will go up significantly.

So, figure this part of product development will cost you around $3000 per batch.

While $3000 doesn't seem too bad, the product development costs are not done yet. If you are serious about running a cosmetic business you MUST test your products to ensure they are safe and effective. Preservative Efficacy Testing is a must. It can be a little pricey to start out if you have multiple products, but the one-time cost of this (~$600/product) is far less than payment on a lawsuit. Sensitivity testing should be done too, but can be optional, if your budget is super tight. However, if the product is going to be applied near the eyes or has ingredients like SPF, AHAs or BHAs, etc, you should really consider budgeting this in. If you are going into bigger retail stores or on TV selling, some will require you to have RIPT done. These tests start at $900 and go to $1500. If you're selling an SPF product, don't forget that SPF testing will probably cost you around $5000-$8000. Note these are ballpark figures.

So, the hidden costs of formula development have now pushed your cosmetic start-up costs to about $10,000 minimum.

Now, we have not even talked about formula ownership! Up until this point, we are going the least expensive way- working with the contract manufacturer and using their lab for formulas and manufacturing. This route, initially can save you some money. However, if you are interested in selling your brand at some point, you will need to own the formulas or your brand does not own any intellectual properties. Some manufacturers can be negotiated to give you the formula but often after a significant amount of sales. After all, the factory will want to LOCK YOU IN so they can continue to be profitable. If you own your formula, you have the freedom of going to bid at another factory and achieve some potential savings. Better yet, if you own your formula and the formula is truly unique, you potentially can patent the formulation and have an unique selling preposition. How do you own a formula? This is when you will have to hire a formulation consultant.

Cosmetic business costs

Besides the cost of product development, there are basic costs associated with owning a cosmetic business. If you are going to sell cosmetics and you don't want to lose everything, you should incorporate. In the US you could conduct your business under a Sole Proprietorship, but this makes you completely liable for anything bad that might happen as a result of your products. You would be risking your savings, your car, and your home. You do not want to do this. Incorporate to protect your personal assets from liability. This will cost you about $500.

Business Insurance

Now, you also need to be considered – Property Insurance and General Liability Insurance. Property insurance is just that – it protects your property, like rental insurance would. In the event of, let's say, a fire, everything related to the retail aspect of your business (computers, your product inventory) are covered. The insurance company will write you a nice, big check for what you lost. This insurance is a great idea for a skincare or hair care company, in the event of misfortune, but if your budget is tight, it is probably not necessary. Formulators and manufacturers don't necessarily have to have this one, but again, it's a good idea.

Anyone serious about a cosmetic business should have is general liability insurance. And, unfortunately, this is the expensive one. This insurance is in the event that someone experiences an adverse reaction to your product, or slips and falls on your property. The cost of this insurance is typically based on how much sales your business has during the year. The limits are set so that the insurance company will pay a total of X amount of dollars (general aggregate limit), and will only pay a certain number of occurrences or claims. The higher your sales, limits, and occurrences, the higher the monthly premium, formulators should have this insurance in case their formulation is the reason for the occurrence and likewise for manufacturers – if something they did during the manufacturing process contaminates the product and causes the adverse reaction, they are responsible.

Sometimes, if you work with contract manufacturers and or contracted formulators they will "umbrella" the cosmetic company on their policy. This means that the manufacturer or formulator's insurance company is including your products on the insurance. It does not mean that you are insured individually as a cosmetic company. That is why it is important for your company to have its own insurance. Formulators and manufacturers can be insured until kingdom come, but ultimately responsibility falls on the company for the safety of the products. If the product doesn't perform the advertised claim, or you do something to make the product unsafe, you are responsible. Selling homemade products is a huge risk – and any adverse reaction can potentially cost you thousands or millions. So, you just have to weigh the odds.

If your dream is to get your product into a large retailer – most major companies require proof of insurance before selling your product, as they will assume no liability. Insurance costs will depend on lots of factors but a rough estimate is ~$300 per month per $1,000,000 of insurance.

There are lots of other business related costs such as fees for lawyers, accountants, employees and taxes but the details will be highly dependent on where you are located and how you run your business. You should just figure on some number for business costs like these.

Marketing & Sales Costs

The final area of start-up costs that we'll cover is your marketing costs. This represents any money you put out to develop and sell your product. If you begin an online business (which is what we would suggest) the initial costs can be fairly low. Running a website can be done for less than $500 a year. Online promotion can be done for next to nothing and requires mostly an investment of your time. The amount of time you dedicate to online marketing will directly relate to how much product you sell. More time generally will mean greater sales. The activities that you do would be writing blog posts about your topic, participating in social networking sites, commenting on other people's sites, and conducting online auctions.

Filling orders will be your next significant cost. You will need to have money available for boxes for shipping, people to actually fill the orders and shipping costs. When you are coming up with the price of your product don't forget to include shipping as part of your costs. This can often be as much or more than the cost of the product. For example, if it costs you $3 to make your product, shipping costs will easily be $3 so you need to charge $6 per unit just to break even.

Another option is to get a booth at a local market and sell your products directly. Booth costs vary but you can get some for between $50 and $125 a day. If you can sell more than that in a day then you're making a profit. Once you've established your brand you may also attempt to get your product sold by some of the local shops in your area. For hair care brands, go see if your local salon will carry your brand. For skin products, perhaps a local spa or specialty gift shop would carry your products. You will have to give up a significant amount of your direct sell profit but you'll ideally make it up with a high volume of sales.

Cosmetic Business Start- up Costs

A cosmetic business can be profitable but it is much more complicated than making a lotion in your kitchen and selling the product to a demanding public. When you figure in the costs of product development, business, and marketing you realistically need about $15,000 – $20,000 to invest up front. Once you start making sales you can make that money back but understand that this is the minimum amount you are going to need to get started.

CONCLUSION

Starting your own unique cosmetics business from home is probably one of the easiest ways to becoming a part of this multi-billion dollar growing industry.... over 7 billion actually. New cosmetic lines are opening up shop every day, and with the internet reach, many are cashing in on their creativity and passion. The caveat is not everyone can make it. While the industry seems glamourous and profitable, you really have to love it to be in it. After all, it is the "WHY ARE YOU IN THIS" going to be your motivation to have your own beauty business, in fact for any business. Remember the saying- Love what you do and you never work a day.

Want more? You can contact me via my website www.gracekingdombeauty.com or send me an email to ginger@gracekingdombeauty.com

Good luck to your adventure!

Grace Kingdom Beauty

Creating Beauty From Concept To Counter